D1610179

Gallery Books
Editor: Peter Fallon

THE SHELTERED NEST

Seán Dunne

THE SHELTERED NEST

Gallery Books

The Sheltered Nest
is first published
simultaneously in paperback
and in a clothbound edition
in March 1992.

The Gallery Press
Loughcrew
Oldcastle
County Meath
Ireland

ISBN 1 85235 084 9 (*paperback*)
     1 85235 085 7 (*clothbound*)

The Gallery Press receives financial assistance from An Chomhairle
Ealaíon / The Arts Council, Ireland.

Contents

I stood among my own,
Not under foreign skies
Or sheltered by foreign wings,
And I survived that time, that place.

— Anna Akhmatova

The Abdication

She sat in a summerhouse in Tipperary
In the nineteen thirties, weighed
By a gymslip and headband.
Couples chattered on a shaved lawn.
Jewels and glasses were twinkling stars
In songs her sister sang before sleep.
She spread a newspaper across pleats.

Steady as a stick in search of water,
Her fingers edged along lines of print:
Scandal, divorce, crisis, shock,
Each word a seismic secret found out.
The world went still as cut-outs.
A globe slipped from its axis in a classroom.
The world fell loose and open like a dress.

The Word Collectors

1

They listened like informers,
Gathering words to please the keen
Priests and teachers,
Students with hands soft as damask.

In an old book, their phrases seem
Speech-seeds spilling from mouths,
Dust swept from a shelf collapsing
Beneath rusted iron and broken tools.

Their names are rows of headstones,
A casualty list from the Somme or Dunkirk.
All that's left of them is print.
Everything about them is silence and ink.

2 *Irish*

after Donal Ó Liatháin

I am a cargo ship in full sail
With no harbour in sight.
I am a book no one understands
In a language from the sky.
I am a lamp lit in a cupboard
With all the doors shut tight.

Must I stay hemmed like a ship in a bottle,
Escaping like a whisper all my life?
Or will the key of Christmas flick
The lock free and let me sail
At last across the threshold?

Refugees at Cobh

We were sick of seeing the liners leave
    With our own day in, day out, so when
The boats edged with refugees to Cobh
    It was worth the fare to travel
From Cork to glimpse them on railed decks.
    They seemed like ourselves,
Their clothes were different:
    Dark coats and scarves like shawls,
Shoes heavy as anvils. Their talk
    Thickened: accents the sound of rocks
Crumbling and crunching in quarries.
    We pushed pins in the maps
Of their towns and regions,
    A homeland rife with altered borders.
They hadn't a word of English but we gave
    What we could: sheets and rationed tea,
Sweets, blankets, bread, bottles of stout.
    The night they sang for hours
We heard their music pour over the islands,
    And none of us recognised the words.
I still see the lights of Haulbowline
    Shimmering as verses broke among waves
And then moonlight fell on silence.

    So strange to see emigrants to Ireland
Huddled near posters telling us to leave
    The broken farms for New York streets.
It was our Ellis Island: hunched
    Lines of foreigners with bundles

Staring at the grey cathedral, the terraces
   Of houses curved like icing around
Hills where handkerchiefs fluttered.
   In time we turned them away. Most stood
As still as cattle when the ship drew out
   And the pilot boats trailed after it.

The Blackbird

after the Irish, twelfth century

A blackbird breaks the silence
With frantic cries of grief.
His nest is torn and trampled,
The bones of his young are scattered.

Frail bird, I'll tell you this:
I know something of what you feel.
When it comes to hurt in homes
There's little for you to teach.

A lout climbed up and smashed
Your home and heart in a flash.
The careful curves of your nest
Are just twigs to a man like that.

Your little ones came when you called,
Clustered on a steady branch.
Not one of them needs you now:
Nettles thrive where you sang.

Your mate was beside you always,
Her beak a bright nib of light
When that man sprung his trap
And she died, her wings sapped.

I find it hard, dear God, to live
With all that you make happen.
It sometimes seems that others thrive
While all I build lies in tatters.

Grief holds me like a shawl
Weighing me down as I walk.
Nothing I say can change things.
Nothing can mend that wounded branch.

The Sentence

after Akhmatova's Requiem

The word was a stone that fell
On my breast that's heaving still.
It was no surprise when spoken
And I'll get by, whatever the case.

I'm up to my eyes in things to do:
Anything that kills memory and pain,
Anything that makes my heart a stone
And still explains how to live again.

Summer will traipse in and insist
On dancing and sun despite my mood.
I knew this a long time ago:
A brilliant day and a deserted house.

The Sheltered Nest

My sadness is a mottled bamboo.
Roots twist in torment underneath
But even before the first shoot grew
It contained a pattern of future tears.

Why bother now wipe stains from clothes?
I walk without hope by the Lee and Suir.
An old book in my hand shields me
From sunlight breaking over Inchigeela.

Bottles and bags among weeds on the Lough,
Sparrows in gardens along Glasheen Road.
I watch rain speckle grey waters,
Birds pass in pairs with heads bowed.

The photographs are taken from walls
Leaving wallpaper lighter where they were.
I feel a new space darkening like the mark
Where once a wedding ring was worn.

Day after day the gardens bloom.
Fuchsias pop open in my children's hands.
How long now before my heart's threads
Float with gossamer tugged from hedges?

From Hackett's Terrace I survey quays.
No sirens sound through dead factories.
Moonlight invades a ruined playground
As I count the bridges from here to home.

When least expected I found love again,
Startling as a bracelet gleaming in grass.
At odds with no one, I found ease
And shed my sadness, a stained suit.

In Gougane Barra at the end of autumn
There's little sign of the grass wilting.
I think of that crossing North Gate Bridge
And of a woman waiting, red hair unpinned.

Surf breaks with driftwood near Ballymore.
Our children skim stones on rough water.
Shadows play on a black flute
As you lean into winds filled with warning.

My tongue on your tongue is the touch
Of leaf against leaf on a twisted tree.
Your breasts are fruit falling as your arms
Shelter the frail nests of my cares.

Pictures from an Exhibition

for Tomáisín Ó Cíobháin

Ball Uisce

A limb of water in Connemara
— A liquid arm in a socket of peat —
Glistens on a canvas and curves
Like a lover's arm relaxed in sleep.

The sky is a swollen tent of rain.
Gathered storms darken clouds.
The arm stirs when brushed by winds
That skim the stretched meniscus.

The Blaskets

There's no one now to write down
The story of homes reduced to husks.
Who knows the folklore of a ruin
Or the triad of a caved-in roof?

The last ones walk through Dunquin
As if still on the island paths —
A straight line behind each other,
A list of words for the one thing.

Old Fields

The lines between them are threads
Sewn to fasten the hillside down.
Old beehives in the sun, huts
Bulge in corners where sheep stand.

Sheets flap between them and the road,
Laundry waving in starched surrender.
If split any more, those fields will be
Only stones in pockets for eldest sons.

Grandfather's Glasses

They made him look like Gepetto
Who made Pinocchio in the story-book,
His bald head bent over worked wood.
Years after he died, I found them

Among pension books and lighters,
Flints that smelled vaguely of him.
The handles were frail threads
When I drew them apart and held

A smudged lens to the kitchen light.
I fixed them on before his mirror,
Rust nicking the back of my ear;
His thin face formed in a watery blur.

Sydney Place

Beans

What must they have grown to now,
Secrets sprouting in the dark?
My arm resting on a windowsill,
I flicked mung beans at ivy
As if next morning I'd wake
To a beanstalk ripe with solutions.

The Mobile

It jangles in a mild breeze
Above my son tucked in his cot.
Each morning he wakes and strains
To reach its impossible height,
But misses always those turning birds,
Plastic fish swimming in the sky.

Railings

My son swings from black railings
Where once a horse was tethered.
Snow settles on his woollen hat,
Crystals dissolve in strands.
In a photograph he squints ahead
To a future from which we've gone.

The Dead Pianist

The pianist's funeral passes
Terraces at evening, his long
Fingers joined on a still stomach.
I think of John Field dead in Moscow
And hear a nocturne settling
In leaves from trees on Wellington Road.

The Bus Station

The passport photo booth flashes
In the bus station near the river.
I watch it from my high window:
A message sent with a mirror
From desperate souls in a valley,
Frantic for answers in the far hills.

The Poet Upstairs

The poet is working upstairs.
I can hear his typewriter clattering
Between our arguments, poems made
Among shouts and accusations:
Our fierce anger a dust that clogs
The bright needle of his work.

Tea

Endless infusions, silver strainers.
Teapots, bags dangling from strings
In cups where dried leaves darken.
Rosehip and hibiscus, camomile, mint,
And lapsang souchong with its smell
Of woodsmoke from a forest hearth.

The Lost Wife

A poet by the fireside cries
For his dead wife. Whiskey draws
Sadness from him like a keen.
He talks of voice, hair, skin,
Holds a ring up to the light
And frames the space where she has been.

The Parade

A window opening on a parade,
Brass pounding in McCurtain Street.
Drums reverberate and boom
The rhythm of a New Orleans funeral,
Dancers behind a coffin, pearl
Teeth flash against the sun.

Dried Flowers

They crackle when I press them
In a vase on the grey mantelpiece,
Their country colours stranded
Among ashtrays and lampshades.
They are frail fossils left behind,
Crisp hopes weathered and worn.

The Old School

The school is gone from Belgrave Place,
Rats scramble in briars near the wall.
A light burns in a closed classroom
Where I sense the ghosts of children,
Their pinafores pressed and the lost
Future a blackboard at which they stand.

The Night Sky

A moon you could hang a coat on,
A pantomime curve in the sky.
Smog rises above roofs of the city
From homes rife with offerings
To appease it before it disappears:
The last god going in a sliver of light.

The Last Toast

after Akhmatova

I toast our wrecked home,
The sadness of my life.
I raise my glass to you
And the loneliness we shared,

And to mouths that betrayed us,
To cold eyes without a hint of pity,
To the brutal world and the fact
That God, even God, hasn't saved us.

The Stone Carver

for Ken and Rachel Thompson

PRAY FOR ME, ERIC GILL, STONE CARVER 1882-1940,
AND FOR MY MOST DEAR WIFE, MARY ETHEL 1878-1961.

1

They carried your coffin in a cart
Across the Chilterns. Wheels left
Tracks you'd once have treasured.
You lay in straw as in a manger,

Dear Mary's kiss the last on your lips
That knew so many and spoke
Of Christ's genitals as a fondled form.
Old cock-of-the-walk, sex was a feast

Of trussed skirts and crumpled aprons,
A quick gift gathered in stable or bed.
The papers now would call you a beast:
Sex-crazed stone man is finally dead.

2

You treated stone with a lover's tact,
Edges peeled back like a thick
Jumper raised as static sparkled

And you reached the last lines,
Tilting the thin chisel's tip.
Dust fell like a cloud of underclothes.

3

Part of you preferred things plain,
To fashion always with strict delight,
Like the breadboard you made and set
With nicked edges on a kitchen table,

Crumbs scattered where tea-towels
Were shaken when loaves cooled
As if any moment crowds would come
Ravenous from Mass on Sunday morning

And Mary's bell clang in the yard,
Her hair a combed river of lines
You'd soon chisel in blocks of wood,
Her apron warm and smelling of bread.

Altnasheen

Altnasheen, the gorge of the fairies, may ultimately vanish altogether as a name, for names live only as long as people have a use for them.
— Michael Viney, *The Irish Times*

The black sewing-machine rusted
Among bushes at Altnasheen,
Blackcurrants clustered around it
Where a faded *Singer* peeled.

White sheets flapped on a line
To signal to cousins come visit,
Calling cards fluttering,
Handkerchiefs from a train.

I have never gone there but hear
Altnasheen unravelling on a page,
A creel of sound that I carry,
Laundered linen to sort through.

I listen to its music and know
The treadle trapped by a stone.
Near it, a mouth wide in silence,
The curved horn of a gramophone.

The Pursuit of Arethusa

Jaded from chasing through woods all day,
I still found time to love the way
Light spilled between leaves as if poured
From a spoon tilted over the trees.
Pathways crackled with dried leaves
And twigs that snapped while birds
Scattered before me like torn words.

Hair blew in my face, its curls combed out.
In pools I watched it quiver but thought
It hardly a thing to write home about.
Men whispered in its strands after feasts,
Grinning with gristle between their teeth.
Not all nymphs are open like a text.
That day I yearned for water, not sex.

I wanted torrents to pour past my lips.
The forest was a stifling warmth, its heat
A clinging shawl from head to feet.
My world shrank to a need to drink
When I came to a stream and entered it.
I could count stones on its clear bed
Where minnows moved in a darting script.

I looked around: not a soul; I peeled
My clothes away and sensed something turn
Quieter than shadows across an urn.
Water clamped my ankles as I stood
In terror, tightening like a rinsed sheet.

I plunged when knives of sunlight cut
Lines through water that broke and shook.

I heard a voice boom out my name.
Alpheus, god of the river, manic
Like a dirty old man at night
Watching women wash by candlelight.
I sensed his fierce desire unfurl
As I crossed my arms in panic
And ran: a panting, frightened girl.

I ran so fast my skin dried in seconds.
I could barely breathe: the world spun
In a spume of names on my tongue —
Orchomeneus, Psophis, Maenalus, Erymanthus.
I blurted a list of syllables and sounds
When he rushed across the quivering ground,
His breath on my neck, his hands held out.

A child grasping a hem, I cried
To Diana, pleading that this god
Dissolve in streams and pools.
A cloud formed in a sudden mist.
I entered it as if through a gate,
My limbs frozen as a roof under frost.
I was a hidden hare while hounds rage past.

He followed my steps to the last trace
Where the clouds began. I knew from his face
It was all over. Sweat poured. My teeth
Chattered and my skin went cold. I shook
And wished for the old safety of skirts
In kitchens where women cut meat
Or yelped as I tugged at their sandals.

I edged my foot and trickles gathered.
A pool formed in the clay at my feet.
I turned to water and breached the ground
When he mingled with me and we poured
In darkness until I landed without love
In Ortygia, with a hopeless, artesian sigh.
I hid there for ages, then poured into earth above.

(Ovid, *Metamorphoses, Book V*)

Marginal Man

Thomas Merton 1915-1968

Black and white stranger in a snowy field,
Your gloved hands chop wood with an axe
That cuts through bark with the flat
Thud of steel through silence. A cap
Heavy as a fisherman's circles your head.

Easy for me to think of you tonight
With an Irish wind howling against the glass,
A teapot cooling among sandwiches packed
For children's journeys. Shadows from plants
Trail into corners where books are stashed.

Otherwise little to notice but sounds —
Floorboards crackling into place and coals
Collapsing in the grate. A broken tap
Sounds its annoying morse while wind
Whistles around bins in the wet yard.

Silence was the theme you took,
The quiet of places where nothing stirred
But pens on paper in cold scriptoria,
Your knuckles cold as Gallarus or Kells.
Yet still you never let anything go:

Meadowlarks singing in settled snow
Moved you to scribble a margin note
While light on gables in dying fields
At times could answer your deepest need.
And while you worried about the Bomb

Or agonised over a nurse you loved,
A bird seen suddenly over an elm
Became a *koan* containing everything.
The sky at evening was a parchment
Flecked with lines from Japanese prints.

In Washington the meetings dragged
On and on, words snapping like sticks
As maps were altered by a mood. The Pentagon
Was hardly your temple, you who loved the mat
Spread loosely over the earthen floor,

Who loved the simple pot and the sound
Of a camera clicking as you faced the last
Shaker buildings left in cold Kentucky,
Your lens aimed at a broken sash
Or the peeling walls of a house that still

Moved you, its message one you understood.
You were outside everything, marginal man,
Forever on the edge with the necessary trash
Of poems or silence, content to watch geese,
Or light blazing into a teeming barn.

I keep your picture in my crowded room.
What worth your silence or your quick death,
Your side scorched and the electric fan
Tangled on the floor, your bare feet wet?
The monk is a bird who flies very fast.

Locusts sounding among sycamores,
Light was shaken between rows of pines.
Snow fell lightly as a brushstroke
In the cold dusk when they buried you.
You who wrote of the need for peace

Came home in an army plane. The teapot's cool.
The fire guts out and the house is still.
A cat cries out in a neighbour's yard
And trawlers turn towards flares at sea.
The world in the end comes down to these.

Wood-gatherer in a snowy field,
You pose on logs in rolled-up sleeves,
A Buddha at ease. Your silence spreads.
The raw gales rip yachts from moorings.
The morning's thaw is a new page turning.

'Easter Snow'

for Nuala O'Connor

When I heard that slow air first
Its name held me in a warm glove.
It slipped from a flute, ascending
Slowly: a bird with torn feathers.

Seamus Ennis loved it and played
Over a waiting grave in Clare.
A piper in his coffin was tapped
By turned earth as the song rose.

Later, in the Naul, it was played
Near another grave while Seamus lay
In his own coffin waiting,
His long fingers stiff and cold,

The song played over as if
At Easter by a graveside waiting
For the hedges to empty of all
But firm eggs tucked in snow.

Wittgenstein in Ireland

He could only think clearly in the dark
So he came to Ireland, scouring Dublin
And Wicklow for shelter where thought
Might sprout in the night, a frail mushroom.

Near Arklow he wrote in a sunlit ledger.
A girl eavesdropped on pages and found
Only long words, the *Schauung* and *ich*
Of whatever it was he was up to.

In Connemara, he found the last pool
Of darkness in Europe, a clarity in rock
Reached like the root of a stubborn word.
Clear as theorems, sentences formed.

On an old dictionary, his simple truth:
*The limits of my language are the limits
Of my world*, and around it silence:
A homeland everywhere, to make his own.

Marmalade and Mrs Mandelstam

Thank you, my dear. Marmalade, it is my childhood.
—Nadezhda Mandelstam to Bruce Chatwin

To please Nadezhda in her old age
It was useless to spout in liberal rage.
Marmalade, thrillers, the best champagne,
Drew more response than relived campaigns.

Marmalade especially won her over:
A taste of life as teeming pleasure.
Its smell was girlhood, secure as shavings
Curled in a schoolbag on winter evenings.

When policemen ripped her rooms apart
For poems and books, they ignored the jar
That bound her to the world as much
As words transformed by poetry's touch

And drove her on when all seemed waste
But for the memory of that redemptive taste.

Eldress Bertha and the Apples

She sang for the day that was in it. The last one left, she wrote down the recipes from her Shaker world and made a book. It matched the chairs and sideboards of her sect, each recipe plain as a table. Each line was what it was and nothing more, lying on its own like the lines of a poem. She sang when her hands plunged into basins of cool flour. Husks of corn lay on a table. Watermelons too, the pips spat out by men after work. Children ate small tomatoes whole and the juice ran down their chins. She grew cabbages and carrots, peppers and musk melons, garlic, potatoes, peas. When she made a salad, she worked with the care of a quiltmaker, setting each chopped and diced thing down until a bright assembly filled the plate.

It was apples she loved most. She said their names as if they were the names of children. Talman Stuarts, she would say, they're for the summer. And Yellow Transparents, they suit the summer as well. Maiden's Blush now, that's more for the spring. We boil Jonathans in the fall and Winesaps go well then too. We use the Nonesuch for mincemeat pies, she would say, and Sheep's Nose and Turkey Egg apples. And for Shaker hand pies we use the Chenango or Virgin apple.

Then she sang for the day that was in it and her song stayed in the minds of those who heard it and remembered it always, as they might remember a flour-stain on an old recipe book or the lingering smell of cider in a cask.

The Last Shakers

They wear round glasses and bonnets
Like extras on the edge of a Western,
Settled in words from Custer's time:
Womenfolk, homestead, frontier.

The chairs they occupy will go
At auction when the last eldress dies,
And their houses, fresh as brochures,
Will sell in nostalgia for another age.

I can warm to that spare, ascetic
Achievement: order, not ornament,
In details of chairs or woven rugs,
Everything finished with a grace

That makes the perfect seem natural.
They surface in *Time* or *Life*: one-page
Appeasements of an unnamed instinct,
The last old women serene in porticoes.

As you sat watching a programme
Where the twelve survivors spoke,
(Your thin-rimmed glasses like theirs),
Knitting a mustard-coloured jumper,

Everything about you merged with them —
Even your hair bunched back with pins —
Until I thought you'd suddenly shake
Flour from an apron and pine for plains.

The Jewish Museum in Portobello

Ireland, they say, has the honour of being the only country which never
persecuted the jews. Do you know that? No. And do you know why?...
— Why, sir? Stephen asked, beginning to smile.
— Because she never let them in, Mr Deasy said solemnly.
                                        — James Joyce, *Ulysses*

Two candles on a kitchen table,
Glazed bread beneath a cloth.
You lean against cool walls
As if to dodge a searchlight.

Edelstein? Your name's Edelstein?
Exile hovers around your name —
All that's left of your lost father
Fleeing from Nazis in Dortmund.

Shreds of barbed wire from a camp,
A swastika on a polished badge.
Give me instead old Mushatt the chemist,
His balms and potions to ease a graze.

We stand before unrolled scrolls,
Our fingers laced like plaited loaves.
I see you pleading behind camp gates,
Your hair flung among the hair of thousands.

Your father is a quiet ghost moving
In the sealed ghetto of childhood.
The souvenir mug he gave you survives,
An ark of memory you never forsake.

In Fine's shop in Terenure, I buy
Rye bread, chunks of kosher cheese.
Streetlights are a bright menorah
Lit with singing for our feast.

Your father lacked Abraham's luck,
Abandoned by angels on the Sabbath.
His loss is a closing of synagogues,
The fading of black from prayer-straps.

We kiss under a canopy of clouds,
Closer than a skull-cap to its skull.
Loss is a covenant between us,
The burnt bread of your father's exile.

The Gougane Notebook

A rainbow over the lake
   cataracts on hillsides
      bright as bracelets

Trees against mountains
   a darting bird caught
      in calligraphy's fleck

After a white wedding
   confetti speckles gravel:
      paint splashed on stones

Pine trees after a storm:
   pencils strewn from a bag
      insects nudging the bark

Names of the dead in Irish
   moss on old headstones
      a fur to warm dead script

Candles in an oratory
   cool stone of a font
      rustle of reeds in water

Lovers at hotel windows
   gauze of midges
      and a moon over Allua

The silence that climbs
    these mountains with me
        lightening my luggage

Clear water over stones
    curled horns of a ram
        strands of wool in barbs

Again the falls glisten
    morse sent from hills
        signals I decipher

Ripples where a fish leaped
    its mouth a momentary O
        silent soprano

Colours changing with light
    a coat turned over and over
        canvas brushed in seconds

Snow falling on snow
    lives fluttering to earth
        settling into silence

A broken bell buried in ivy
    its tongue thick with rust
        tone turned to a thud

Stone beds where monks slept
    children hide and seek
        wind whipping with penance

A priest buried on the island
   headlights in a circle on the shore
      to light his coffin on the causeway

My place of hills and silence
   violence in faraway squares
      disruption shuffling the maps

My place of peace in crisis
   a core crumbling around me
      the mountains steady and still

A heron over the lake at evening
   its shadow on the surface
      one incomplete without the other

Flies skitter on the lake's skin
   that stillness my strength
      the waterfall's gathering roar

Doneraile Court

The Awbeg's sheet of glass snaps
And surges forward in shattered foam.
Packaged like a sonnet, the manor stands
In a frozen block of lives and stone.
Its windows mirror the landscape's curve.

A Morris Minor in the gravelled drive
Snorts. Smoke sputters from its exhaust.
It is nineteen forty and Europe's skies
Darken with bombers. Here, churns
Clatter the coinage of creamery returns.

She walks at evening down the steps,
Stilettoes startle birds from trees.
She's home on holiday from the Blitz
To the worn carpets of her Irish home.
She absorbs the agony that we disown

And drives over hillsides to Farahy,
Shaping a story as the car bumps
And headlights catch a fox in cones.
The world is shaped to a cancerous lung.
A wireless crackles news from Germany.

But it's nineteen ninety and I sense
Her imprint on October air.
The land is tense, a stifled scream,
And I walk to ease a fresh despair.
I too could make a river weep

And trees that border my slow walk
Shelter no nymphs or attentive muse.
Trout choke in streams and float
With swollen bellies towards reeds.
No woods can answer and no echoes ring.

A peacock near a sundial spreads
Its feathers to make a fearsome fan.
The lawns are perfect but I walk
With a marriage lost, the papers signed.
I pocket conkers for a waiting child

As a new love forms like a sentence
Carved in a tree, mutability's bole.
Lawns and poems and tales are art
Arranged to shield the breaking heart.
A pigeon coos in a cracked gutter.

Nineteen forty and she stops
Work to look on Ballyhoura hills.
Moths flutter near heavy curtains,
Their flight a torment in the room.
Tomorrow she's off to London again.

Fifty years later, I too return
To children, pages, my waiting home.
I touch red hair and my fingers burn
With ecstasy. Still no woods answer,
No echoes ring among the trees.

Workmen hammer a refurbished hall.
Smooth conveyor, the Awbeg slides past.
Nineteen ninety and I head
For home and the hard century's close,
Turning in darkness where the road goes.

Throwing the Beads

A mother at Shannon, waving to her son
Setting out from North Kerry, flung
A rosary beads out to the tarmac
Suddenly as a lifebelt hurled from a pier.
Don't forget to say your prayers in Boston.
She saw the bright crucifix among skyscrapers,
Shielding him from harm in streets out of serials,
Comforting as a fat Irish cop in a gangster film
Rattling his baton along a railing after dark.

Exile

1 *The Blue Eye*

There's a sea-blue eye that stares
At Ireland drawing away.

It will never look again
At the women of Ireland, or its men.

2 *The Last Leaves*

Autumn starts at the edge of the world,
The curving edge where morning slants.
A curlew cries its tale of home
Shed with blossom and the last leaves.

The Woman's Script

My dropped hairpin glistens
In the stream where he swims.
It trembles when he passes
As I lay trembling once
When he passed like a gust
Across a lotus near a pool.
A heron will wear that pin
Before he braids my combed hair.

Once I was a chorus girl,
Then I came to Royal Wei Palace.
Carried in a carved litter,
I cracked whips as servants bowed.
I wore a peacock brooch with studs
Of diamond in its beak and eyes,
But this became disappointment.
Reading old letters, I longed for Liaotung.

A bird-catcher writes and pleads
That I meet him by the river.
My husband watches as I set
My sadness down in secret script,
Marks like chicken-scratches in clay.
My diary wrapped in silk is a box
To carry a body to its grave.
I am a bucket fallen in a well.

My love lives near Mount T'ai.
I long to go there but fear the road
Where floods pour, avalanches fall.
I lean towards the east
As if by leaning we draw close.
What can I send him? The best jade.
The road is bad, it won't arrive.
I hide my face in a creased fan.

My love lives near Cassia Forest.
I long to go there but fear the deep
Waters of river along the way.
I lean towards the south
And tears stain my stiff collar.
I gather jade plates to send him
But the road is long, they won't arrive.
I hide behind a screen of silk birds.

My love lives at Hanyang.
I long to go there but fear the high
Passes among the mountains.
I lean towards the west
And tears soak my furred sleeve.
I will send him a pair of pearls.
The road is long, they won't arrive.
My heart breaks as I finger sable.

My love lives at Goose Gate Pass.
I long to go there but fear the snow
Smothering the unmapped hills.
I lean towards the north.
He is a fan slipped in a sleeve.
I will send him a tray made of jade.

The road is long, it won't arrive.
I press embroidery to my face.

When I first saw him I shook
As if afraid to drop boiling water.
I longed to be a rush mat
Beneath his bed, or a quilt
To guard him from winter frost.
Powdered, I wait as if he'll come.
I draw pillows close and crave
For rapture to blot out the snow.

Autumn Moon

I had never seen it so close,
The moon over Minane Bridge.
Like a Japanese poet on a path,
I stood and watched as it rose
To the roar of shots and the wild

Yap of hounds with a dropped bird.
Elsewhere armies stalk to war
But I open to small things —
Ditches crunching with frost,
Wheel-ruts in mud, the far

Bark of a dog in a farmyard.
And your smooth, cool face,
The eyes dark under lids
Lowered like a pièta's
Against fields and moon.

Acknowledgements and Notes

Acknowledgement is due to the following publications where some of these poems originally appeared: *The Aisling, The Cork Review, Living Landscape Anthology, Oxford Poetry, The Poetry Ireland Review, Poetry Review, The Steeple, Stet, The Sunday Tribune* and *Triskel Poets*.

A number of poems appeared in *Emigration, Employment and Enterprise*, edited by Joe Mulholland and Dermot Keogh (Hibernian University Press, 1989). Others were included in *Bitter Harvest*, edited by John Montague (Scribners); *The New Younger Irish Poets*, edited by Gerald Dawe (Blackstaff Press); and *Thistledown, Poems for UNICEF*, edited by John F. Deane (Dedalus).

'The Blackbird', accompanied by a painting by Tim Goulding, was inscribed in *The Great Book of Ireland* in 1990.

The Shakers, to whom reference is made in a number of these poems, were members of a small American sect founded in the eighteenth century. The sect, which is now almost extinct, was epitomised by its search for a simple life. Its members enjoyed dancing and plain cooking. Their distinctive furniture is highly prized.

page 53 On paper fans and in cloth-bound diaries, women in ancient China wrote their secrets in a language no man could understand. ✶